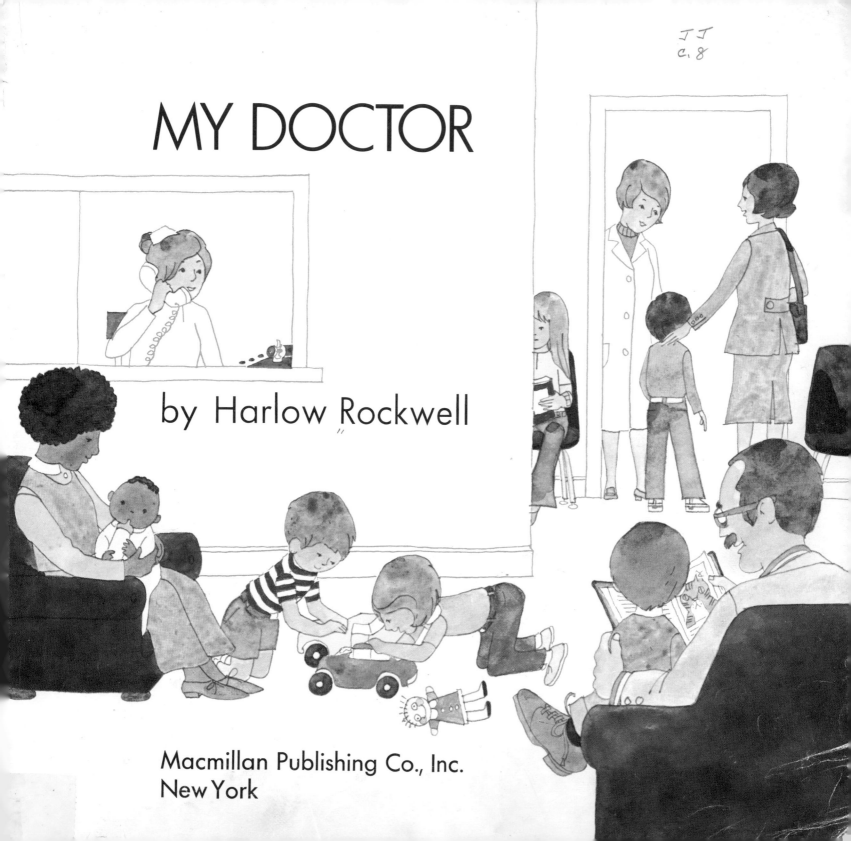

MY DOCTOR

by Harlow Rockwell

Macmillan Publishing Co., Inc.
New York

6 7 8 9 10

The pictures in this book are full-color watercolor paintings. The typeface is Futura Book, hand set.

Library of Congress Cataloging in Publication Data

Rockwell, Harlow.
    My doctor.
    1. Medicine—Juvenile literature.   [1. Medical care]   I. Title.
R130.5.R6   616   72-92442   ISBN 0-02-777480-5

for
Oliver

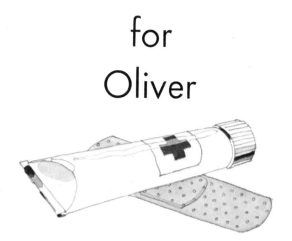

At my doctor's office it is clean and bright.
She has a sink to wash her hands.

There is a scale to weigh me
and to measure
how tall I've grown.

My doctor has a stethoscope.
She listens to my heart beating and
my lungs breathing while I take
a big breath.

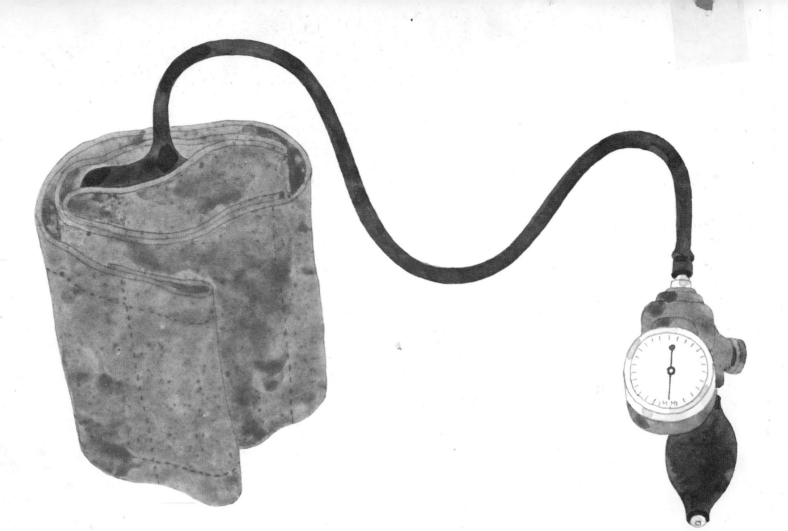

There is a cloth to wrap around my arm.
My doctor squeezes a little rubber bulb
until the cloth is full of air.
It squeezes my arm tight.

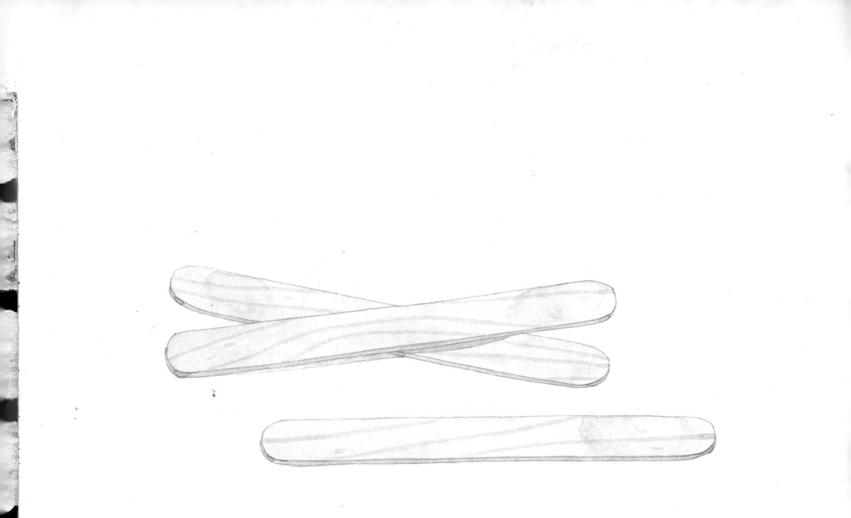

She has wooden tongue depressors to hold
my tongue down when she looks at my throat.

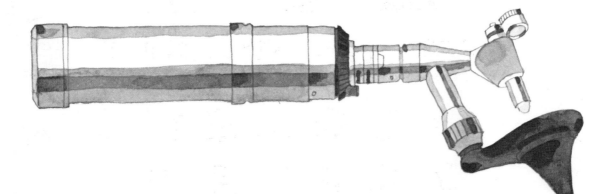

She has a little light.

She looks up my nose and in my ears.

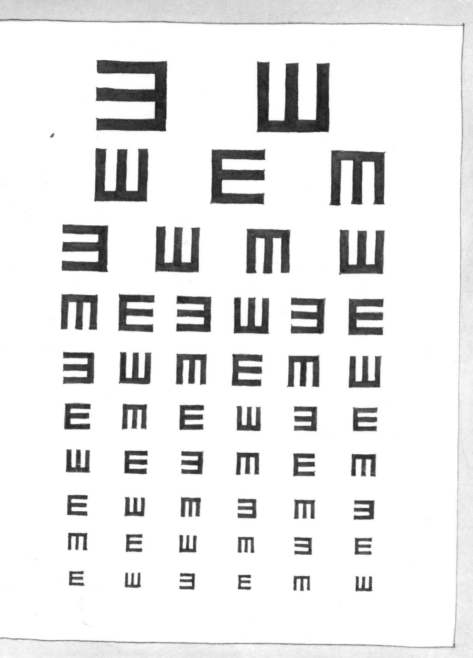

There is an eye chart for me to look at.

My doctor has a long table
with clean white paper on it.

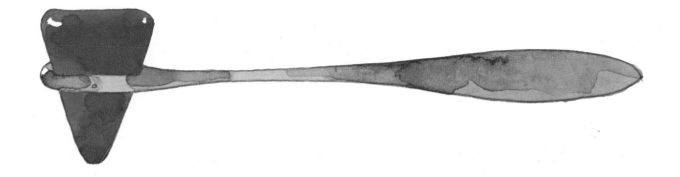

She has a rubber mallet to tap my knees

I lie down
while she feels
my stomach.

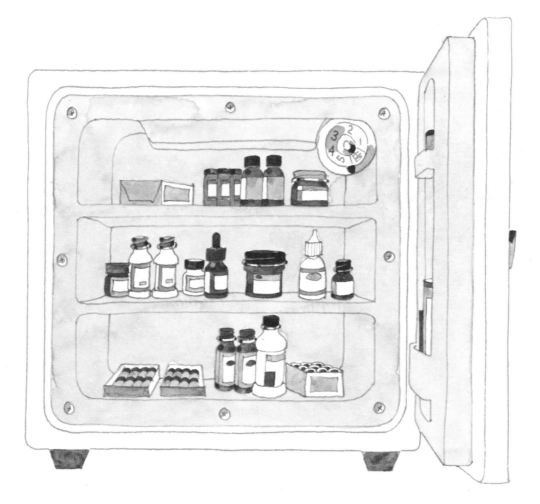

and a small refrigerator full of medicine.

She has a thermometer

and bandages.

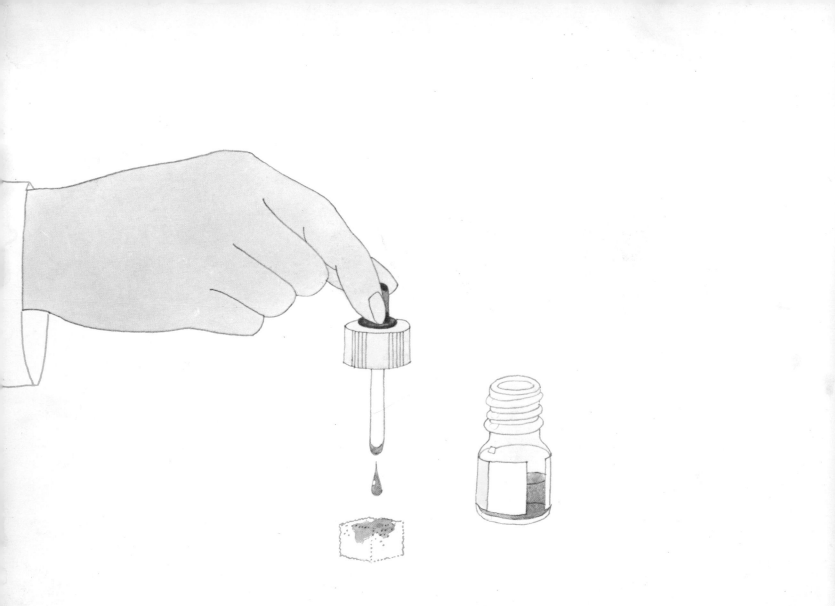

She gives me some red medicine
on a sugar cube. I eat it.

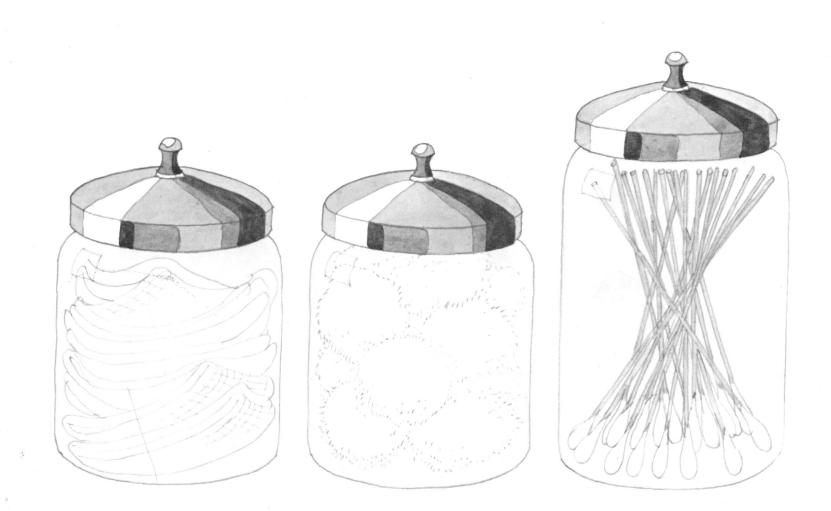

There are jars full of
gauze pads and cotton balls
and cotton swabs on skinny wooden sticks.

There is a bottle of alcohol.

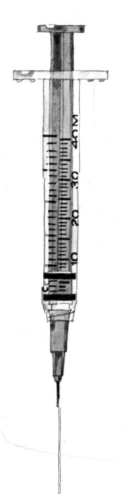

She has a needle to give shots.
But I don't need one today.

My doctor wears
a long white coat.
She keeps her stethoscope
in her pocket.